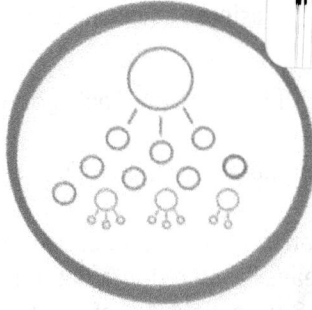

THE COMPLETE NETWORKER

business common sense for network marketers

First Edition

Jason Wells AND **Chris Lopez**

www.MLMCompletePackage.com

The Complete Networker: Business Common Sense for Network Marketers by Jason Wells and Chris Lopez

Published by MLM Complete Package Books, Reno, Nevada.

MLM Complete Package Books
316 California Ave #767
Reno, NV 89509
775.298.1464
http://www.MLMCompletePackage.com

Cover Design: Jason Wells, MLM Complete Package Books
ISBN-10: 0989648338
ISBN-13: 978-0-9896483-3-2

For general information on our other products and services or for technical support please contact MLM Complete Package at 775.298.1464 or http://www.MLMCompletePackage.com

Contents

Preface

Are You Ready To Add Some Common Sense to Your MLM Business?

Our style for building MLM is radically different from other people's in the MLM Industry. It's often described as "going against the grain." Our MLM building techniques may make you question what your upline, company, and all these MLM "gurus" have taught you. But when there is a high failure rate in MLM with those B.S. tactics, going "against the grain" is probably the smartest thing you can do.

Before we jump into all the details, we want to share some background information on ourselves:

- We've been with the same network marketing company for over 10 years each and have been making a full time residual income for the majority of those years.

- Over the years we've received awards for top growth, top sponsors, and major rank advancements - to name a few. We've also earned numerous trips, VIP retreats, cruises, and all the other fun incentives that MLM has to offer.

- More importantly, our downline has been able to do the same thing. Duplication is where the big money is made.

- Thousands of distributors in our company who are not in our downline have come to us to learn our techniques. Simply put, our techniques get real results... without all the MLM B.S.

- Our system, marketing techniques, and training methods have been emulated and copied by people in our company and all around the MLM Industry.

- Teams and companies have offered us multiple six figures to buy our system over the years. In fact, start-up MLM companies have offered top distributor positions to us if we joined and brought over our system. However, we never once took people up on these offers. What we have is too important.

- Our training, marketing techniques, and system are so effective that small businesses and the "traditional" world have approached us for help. How often do you hear about the "traditional" world wanting something from the MLM industry?

- We are Google Adwords Certified. We know of no other network marketing expert who has that certification. That certification is one reason we're able to advertise while the vast majorities of others get banned or "Google Slapped."

It's been very rewarding to see how much our knowledge and expertise have helped our downline, other distributors around our company, and people all around the MLM industry. You're probably wondering, "How did you two guys accomplish all of this?"

Understand that we didn't magically wake up with all of this knowledge one morning. We ran into many of the problems that MLM distributors encounter. We overcame all of these obstacles and wrote this book to help you build a successful network marketing business, as we did, by becoming a Complete Networker. A Complete Networker is someone who has the skills and knowledge necessary to build an MLM business by using "business common sense."

Introduction
About The Complete Networker

You're probably reading this book and have a small but nagging voice in the back of your mind saying, "I don't know if I have what it takes..." How do we know about "the voice?" Well, we have experienced that same voice. It's entirely possible to follow our advice and have the same success that we have had over the years and duplicate it in your MLM business.

MLM doesn't favor one person over another person. **It favors people who put in the work.** No one is born great at building a network marketing organization. Nothing at birth gives one baby a better chance at success in MLM than another baby. Now, if you want to play professional basketball in the NBA, then obviously being 6'10" will make it a lot easier than being 5'10"! But, thankfully, MLM is not that way. That is one of things that makes MLM great.

If there ever was **a secret to success in MLM**, it is to treat your MLM business like a traditional business. Now before you yell,

"Well, Chris and Jason, I already know that! My upline has told me to treat it like a business and not a hobby." We're saying something completely different than the MLM mantra of "treat your business like a business and not a hobby." That mantra is used because they don't know how to train you. They tell you to build more belief, say affirmations all day long, and just "show the plan, show the plan, and show the plan"!

Yuck.

Stop for a minute and name one business that tells its employees the stuff that MLM leaders tell their downline. We can't think of one. Whether you're an Apple fan or not, you have to respect how they revolutionized so many aspects of the computer industry. Now, can you imagine Apple telling its employees to "Make a list of friends and family, get excited about the product, and go out there and make it happen!" It's a ridiculous thought. Yet, why is that the norm in MLM?

Because many "gurus" are either negligent or manipulative.

"Gurus" are in quotes because the majority of these self proclaimed "gurus" are clueless when it comes to building their business. But, they sure know how to make themselves appear as a "guru" so you buy from them! Some are negligent because rather than saying "I don't know how to build the business," they just fly by the seat of their pants and repeat what they hear. Others are just down right manipulative. Many MLM leaders and "gurus" just view their downline with dollar signs floating above their heads.

We've been behind the scenes at MLM training events listening to MLM "gurus" do "locker room" talk and brag about how much money they are making off of crap leads they are selling to their downline, or how they "throw new distributors on the wall to see how long they stick" and stay on the product, or if you "sponsor enough losers you'll eventually find a winner." We are not joking. Those are the exact phrases we've heard many "gurus" say.

One could argue that those techniques work because people have had success using them. However, we disagree because people who have morals and genuinely care about other people cannot run their MLM business in such a manner.

One example really stands out and still raises our blood pressure to this day. Years ago we attended a three day MLM "training" in Las Vegas. *Training* is in quotes because it was one of those events where every person spends 30 minutes selling you his "$1,999 magic bullet course." One of these "gurus" was on stage talking about how he became the #1 sponsor in his company by calling Internet leads. He was offering his lead source and techniques to the people in attendance. His hook was having a live call once a month where people could be a "fly on the wall" and listen to him make live calls to his leads.

Sounds good, right? Later that night after the event had ended and everyone had dinner, the "gurus" were at the bar having drinks. Once the drinks started flowing, the truth came out. The "guru" from earlier turned to the owner of a lead vending company and said, "Just make sure when I do this live training call you send me the good leads, not your normal shitty leads. I actually need to talk with leads on the phone so people will buy the leads."

Wow. We were blown away. After hearing that, we made certain that none of our downline or friends in the industry listened to any of those con artists.

There's a dirty secret in MLM: many MLM leaders and gurus make their money by manipulating distributors because they know they can rip them off. MLM distributors are often targeted because they are motivated to have success and take personal responsibility. On the downside, unfortunately, that makes all of us "ripe for the picking" in the eyes of these lowlifes.

If you have been ripped off buying B.S. "guru" gimmicks that haven't worked, **you now know that it was their "strategy" and not YOU that failed**. We share this information with you so you are aware that there are con artists in the MLM industry (more than you probably think), and to also give you hope in your own future success. Now we just have to make sure you have the right information and you'll be on your way to success.

Success in MLM is an equation. Before we go into the nitty gritty details, you need to understand a key element in what makes any successful business person successful. This key element is very much sought after. It's one of the main reasons thousands of people pursue MBA's each year, why corporate executives get paid 7 and 8 figure salaries, and why some consultants can charge $1,000+ an hour.

This key element is the **ability to break down a complicated process into a series of small, simple steps.** Think about this for a minute because many times people do not grasp how powerful this seemingly simple ability is. Let's look at it from a traditional business perspective. How does a business owner or corporate executive improve the business or generate greater profits? Before anyone is fired or hired or new products are researched and developed, every aspect of the business has to be understood. The better the business is "broken down" and understood, the better the decisions and the results. That way everything can be analyzed under a microscope. It's literally a million dollar skill. It's that important.

Before network marketing, Jason ran and grew a very successful law firm in Northern California. This skill of "breaking down" the law firm's operations helped Jason grow and expand the business into new offices and increase cash flow significantly. He knew the business inside and out: he knew what every employee's responsibilities were, the process of taking on a potential new client, juggling hundreds of cases every month, and making sure court deadlines were met. As you can probably imagine, there were a lot of moving parts in running a successful law firm.

Since Jason knew every aspect of the business and was able to take these complicated processes and break them down, it allowed him to grow the business dramatically. Running the law firm also created an enormous amount of stress for Jason. Stress in the legal world can send people to an early grave. Avoiding the stress is one of the main reasons Jason turned to MLM.

Jason was able to easily generate over $100,000 a month in revenue at the law firm. Yet in the early part of his MLM career, he struggled to even make $100 a month! Why did he struggle? Because he was getting fed manipulative B.S. from his upline and "gurus"! One thing that helped Jason achieve success in the law firm was that he was humble and willing to learn from successful people. Jason knew that having an **ego only gets in the way** of having success. He brought the same attitude to MLM and did what his upline and the industry "gurus" told him to do. All the while, he had a nagging voice in the back of his mind questioning the tactics. He thought to himself, "If I ran the law firm like this, I would not only be out of business, but also be sued for malpractice... but I'm new at MLM and I need to learn how it works..."

After about six months of failing at MLM and using the so-called "duplicatable system" from his upline, Jason decided to **buck the MLM B.S.** He broke away from his upline and evaluated the whole MLM business model in the same way he did the law firm. He needed to treat his MLM business like a *traditional* business, just as he did the law firm.

If you have seen the movie *The Matrix* and remember the end where Neo starts seeing the green code of the matrix that allows him to defeat the evil agents... well, Jason had a very similar experience! Once he used his skill to "break down" MLM into an equation, as he did with the law firm, everything became crystal clear as to what he needed to do to achieve success. Building the MLM business suddenly became easy. He started getting results.

Every time he ran into a problem or wasn't sure what he needed to do, he would ask himself, "What would I have done at the law firm?" That one question always led him to an answer or solution. It eventually led him to build a huge MLM organization.

The mantra of the Complete Networker is to use "business common sense" in your MLM business. Memorize that mantra. **Tattoo it to your forehead**. You need to memorize it because it'll help you sift through the B.S. that is rampant in MLM.

Before you say, "Jason, I don't have the experience of running a law firm like you do... I won't know how to answer that question!" Well, don't worry! The rest of this book and the additional resources at our website www.MLMCompletePackage.com will help you.

The Complete Networker is going to teach you the fundamentals of running an MLM business. Once you learn the concepts of a Complete Networker, you'll never be able to sit through another B.S. training conference call again!

Chapter 1

The Fatal Flaw That Will Destroy Any Hope of Residual Income

What is every business built around? It's built around a product, service, or some combination of the two. A business cannot survive unless it has a product or service to offer or sell.

One of the great things about MLM is that we as distributors don't have to worry about creating the product or service. The good MLM companies spend a lot of time and money developing the products or creating the service.

MLM companies actually have two different components:

1) The product or service that consumers buy. It could be nutritional supplements, healthy coffee, cell phone service, or electrical service, to name a few.

2) The business opportunity which allows other people to join your downline and build an MLM organization to reach their financial goals.

MLM companies must have **both** of these components to be legitimate. If an MLM company doesn't have a product or service for consumers to buy, it's an illegal pyramid or Ponzi scheme. If a company doesn't have the "business opportunity" aspect, then they are not an MLM company, since they don't use an independent sales force of distributors! Wrapping your head around having two different components is essential before moving onto the fatal flaw.

We've heard many B.S. pitches for MLM, you probably have too. Does this pitch sound familiar? "This product is the most potent antioxidant in the universe. It comes from the dust of an ancient asteroid that landed deep in the jungles! This product is poised to take over the market place. It's a ground floor opportunity that will make a thousand millionaires over the next ten years!" Obviously, we are mocking a lot of network marketers (and for good reason.) How many times have you heard people say such things?

Distributors rant and rave about how awesome their product or service is and use it to recruit distributors into the "business opportunity" product. Then they sell their new distributor a big startup package and attempt to have that new distributor sell more startup packages to their own new distributors. Yet, when you look around, when is the product being sold? They use this *supposedly* amazing product to get people in the business, but they don't actually sell the product to *real customers*, who are people who just want to buy the product or service but not be in the business. That doesn't make sense!

At many events the top sponsors are paraded around the stage and they drill into you, "If you get six people, then they get six people, and then those people get six people... You'll be driving a Ferrari/BMW/Mercedes in just a few months!" After all, the "money in MLM is made in recruiting."

Let's analyze it with "business common sense." It will make this *fatal flaw of MLM* stand out like a sore thumb. MLM and franchises are very similar. Comparing the two can lead to some great insight into building a successful MLM business.

Imagine if McDonald's did what most MLM leaders do in regards to recruiting franchise owners, but not getting actual customers. The McDonald's franchise sellers go out and talk about how their food is the most amazing food in the world. (Remember, this is just a hypothetical example!) They hype it up and start selling people on buying franchises. They make great money when people buy a franchise because the new franchise owner has to buy all of the necessary equipment and food. Then they go out and sell another franchise and another because people are making so much money by recruiting other franchise owners. But then something bad happens. The franchise owners start having all the food they bought spoil because no one is coming into the store and buying burgers and fries. They are told,

"Don't worry about that. Just focus on selling more franchises. That's where the big money is!" We'll end the example there, because it's getting absolutely ridiculous.

You'll probably agree that it's a ridiculous example looking at McDonald's and other franchises from this perspective. It's easy to say that this example is ridiculous with franchises, yet it's commonplace in MLM. Do you see what we are getting at? Do you notice the fatal flaw now?

The fatal flaw is that there are no real customers in many MLM organizations. A customer is someone who is buying the product or service for the benefit of the product or service, not for the benefit of potentially making money from the business.

"But, my downline are my customers!" No, they aren't. They are buying the product or service, but they aren't real customers. Somehow along the way, manipulative MLM leaders and "gurus" have brainwashed people into thinking that your downline are your customers and they are all you need. What will happen when they don't make money? You'll see then how loyal many of those people are to the product or service! We understand that a certain percentage of distributors (if you have a great product or service) will "become customers for life," regardless of whether or not they make money, but we wouldn't bet our residual income on those people.

Name one non-MLM business that has more franchise owners or store fronts than it does paying customers. There are none outside of the MLM industry! No wonder so many regulatory agencies have struggled with the legitimacy of MLM and many advertisers, such as Google and Facebook, have banned the majority of MLM distributors from advertising on their platforms.

This concept of "focus on recruiting and don't waste your time getting customers" is complete B.S.! Customers are the lifeblood of any business, including MLM. Simply put, if you don't have customers, you don't have a business. There are two reasons why many MLM companies and leaders preach this nonsense:

1. Many network marketing companies don't have a product or service that is good enough to stand on its own merit. If people will only buy the product or service in the hope of making money, then the only option is to sell the business opportunity and recruit distributors.
2. There is a good product or service, but the compensation plan doesn't pay much money for just selling the product or service to customers. This situation forces people to recruit distributors and sell big startup packages in order to make money.

Why is getting customers the *right* way? Building a customer base gives you a legitimate and real business. This excerpt from a Federal Trade Commission (FTC) statement (http://www.ftc.gov/speeches/other/dvimf16.shtm) drives home the point: "Pyramid schemes now come in so many forms that they may be difficult to recognize immediately. However, they all share one overriding characteristic. They promise consumers or investors large profits based primarily on recruiting others to join their program, not based on profits from any real investment or real sale of goods to the public. Some schemes may purport to sell a product, but they often simply use the product to hide their pyramid structure. There are two tell-tale signs that a product is simply being used to disguise a pyramid scheme: inventory loading and a lack of retail sales. Inventory loading occurs when a company's incentive program forces recruits to buy more products than they could ever sell, often at inflated prices. If this occurs throughout the company's distribution system, the people at the top of the pyramid reap substantial profits, even though little or no product moves to market. The people at the bottom make excessive payments for inventory that simply accumulates in their basements. A lack of retail sales is also a red flag that a pyramid exists. Many pyramid schemes will claim that their product is selling like hot cakes. However, on closer examination, the sales occur only between people inside the pyramid structure or to new recruits joining the structure, not to consumers out in the general public."

Many MLM companies unfairly get called pyramid schemes. However, since the FTC considers a lack of retail sales (customers) a red flag for a potential pyramid scheme, you can start understanding why many view MLM skeptically. It's especially easy to understand the skeptics' point of view since the vast majority of MLM training and MLM leaders put very little, if any, focus on building a customer base. Does anyone in your upline talk about getting customers? Does your upline or company have any training on getting customers? Does the MLM culture you're in have any focus on getting customers? If you answered yes to the questions — great! If you answered no to the questions — that should raise a red flag for you.

The FTC statement states that inventory loading is also a red flag for a pyramid scheme. We don't want you to misinterpret that part of the statement. In our experience, they are talking about companies or uplines that sell startup packages costing $3,000 or more. There is no reason for a new distributor to spend that amount of money on product inventory. In fact, it's becoming less important for you to hold large amounts of inventory, especially in the age of Amazon.com where people are accustomed to getting products shipped to their doorstep. Besides, who really wants to be out delivering products to people all the time? We sure don't.

Now we are not against recruiting people or selling the startup packages. Quite the contrary. We are all for recruiting, when it's done the *right* way by building your organization with customers. In fact, between the two of us, we have personally sponsored over 300 distributors. The majority of those distributors joined with a $600 or $1,200 "big" package offered by our company. Startup packages are great because they give new distributors an opportunity to use and become familiar with the product line or services, often at a steep discount. You need to be familiar with your product or service line in order to market it to customers.

The startup packages aren't designed so you can pump more volume by recruiting. Both packages in our company qualify the new distributor for the top compensation structure, which is very important for their income in the long run. Each package gives different products for the new distributor and his family to try. They even have enough product that new distributors can give out samples in order to get customers.

From our commission check perspective, we would love all new distributors to join with the $1,200 package. However, we don't slam that package down people's throats. Rather, based on the person's budget, interest in the products, family size, and goals, the person gets the startup package that is right for him. The person getting the most appropriate startup package, in turn, is the best for our MLM organization in the long run to build residual income. Do what is best for the person and a good commission check will naturally follow.

If what was discussed in this chapter so far hasn't convinced you of the importance of customers, then seeing the impact of customers on your commission check certainly will. **The potential for residual income with customers will make you rethink the entire way you're building your MLM business.** When we first did the math for how much residual income customers can generate, we were blown away. In fact, we did not believe the numbers and checked them again... and then a third time.

We'll walk you through the exercise and numbers that we did with our compensation plan. The goal is to get your attention and show you what building a customer base can do for your business. In our company's compensation plan, 20 customers purchasing about $100 a month in products (the average order size) will generate approximately $400 a month in commission income. Keep in mind that the $400 is not a one time payment, but rather paid every month. It's residual income because our customers buy each month from us. We'd have to recruit two to four new distributors each month just to make a similar income.

While $400 a month is not enough to retire you from your job, it's a solid foundation. Let's look at $400 a month of income from a different perspective. How much money would you need in the bank at 5% to generate $400 a month in interest? You would need $96,000 in the bank to make $400 a month in interest income. We are being very generous with using a 5% interest rate because no bank is offering anywhere near that.

What's easier, getting 20 customers or saving $96,000? Obviously, getting 20 customers is easier.

Now let's add a layer of duplication. In our compensation plan, if we have four distributors who each have 20 customers (plus our original 20), the monthly income is around $2,000. Now we're starting to talk some real money here! That's $24,000 a year of residual income. That's a very good side income and a very realistic one that you or your new distributors could achieve very quickly.

You would need $480,000 in the bank to produce the same income as having 100 customers in your MLM organization. We'll ask again, what's easier, **getting 100 customers from your efforts**

and your downline's efforts or saving $480,000? The answer is obvious.

Now let's add one more layer of duplication to our example. Let's assume that the four distributors each sponsored four distributors and trained them to get 20 customers. There is now a total of 20 distributors and around 400 customers in the MLM organization. The business would generate close to $10,000 a month in income. And that's *residual* income.

You would need $2,400,000 in the bank to generate income from interest to match having 20 distributors and 400 customers. At this point, this is a ridiculous question, but we have to ask it. **Is it easier to get 400 customers in your total organization or save $2,400,000?** Now do you see why we got so excited and triple checked our numbers?

Will you get 400 customers in your organization overnight? Of course not. But after developing your skills as a Complete Networker, you'll be well on your way to getting that many customers in your organization.

The numbers shared are for our company and products. Your company could be more, less, or about the same. Now it's time for you to figure out how much money customers will make for you. For this example, you will need to determine the average order size for customers in your company. You'll also need to do some basic compensation plan math. If you have trouble figuring out these numbers, then work with your upline or call your company's customer service. They should be more than glad to help out.

Step #1: Multiply 20 customers by the average commission you make off personal customers.

20 customers x _____ (Average commission) = _____

Step #2: Assume you recruited four distributors and they each got 20 customers. 4 x 20 = 80. Multiply 80 customers by the commission you make off of your first level of distributors' personal customers.

80 customers x _____ (Average commission) = _____

Step #3: Assume the four distributors you recruited each recruit four distributors. 4 x 4 = 16 new distributors. Assume those 16 new distributors each gets 20 customers. 16 x 20 = 320. Multiply 320 customers by the commission you make off of your second level of distributors' personal customers.

320 customers x _____ (Average commission) = _____

Step #4: Add the income from the 3 steps together.

_____ + _____ + _____ = _____
  Step 1   Step 2   Step 3   Total

You now have an idea of how much money customers can make for you. There are two potential outcomes after doing this exercise: the numbers will either excite you (as they did us) or they'll depress you.

A few years back we got into a conversation with a person in another MLM company. He started picking our brains about how we built our MLM business. We explained the importance of getting customers. He started doing the income figures for his company and customers immediately, just as you did in the above exercise. It was like watching a slow motion wreck. The color and smile drained off of his face. 500 customers would earn him **$9 a month in residual income**. Yes, nine dollars.

He went into denial that his company would only pay him $9 a month in residual income. Then he went home and confirmed the figures. They still came out to $9 a month.

Yikes!

He quickly called his upline. His upline pulled the typical manipulative B.S., "Don't look at that. The real money is in recruiting. Just keep recruiting, and your problems will be solved." Fortunately, since this guy had talked with us, he saw through the manipulative B.S. that his upline was using to brainwash him.

We hate seeing anyone quit MLM. But, seeing people waste their time and efforts on poor business models that don't pay out for getting customers, is even worse. The bottom line is that those companies and methodologies for building are not sustainable in the long run. We don't know what your company pays you. But if it doesn't get you excited, you need to do an analysis and make sure that you are doing what's best for you, your family, and your future financial goals.

Now if the numbers you calculated excite you, then you're about to go on one wild ride with your MLM business. Those numbers will give you sincere confidence and belief about your business and that will come across to people with whom you're talking. You won't have to do the MLM B.S. of "Fake it 'til you make it" or get yourself "pumped up" before you speak with people.

You can tell the difference between a genuine person who really believes in what he is doing versus someone just going through the motions. It almost seems as if the genuine person can say or do no wrong and people will still sign up with him or her. People are attracted to other people who have sincere beliefs. People with sincere beliefs are rare, especially in MLM.

This sincere belief in your business model goes way beyond just selling your product and getting customers. It has a ripple effect on every person that you sponsor and on his success. When you have that genuine belief in your business, your product, and your own ability to get customers, more people will sign up with you. **Guaranteed.**

Once you actually start producing tangible results by acquiring customers and building your customer base, your sponsorship and duplication rate will increase. It's an amazing phenomenon to watch. We have witnessed downline members, who couldn't sponsor a single distributor and were on the verge of quitting, go on a sponsoring spree. They were successful because they built a customer base.

Once you know how to get customers for your products or service, you have a core money making skill that you can teach to your future team members. You'll just radiate more confidence and have more belief in your company and the MLM model. The more sincere confidence and belief you have, the more people you'll sponsor. It's that simple.

Knowing and understanding how much money you make from building a customer base makes the business more real and more achievable. Most MLM opportunity presentations speak in the abstract when it comes to generating income. The specifics of most MLM compensation plans are incredibly confusing, too! Rather than trying to explain the compensation plan (which we never do in a presentation), you can walk the person through the numbers you determined from the exercise. Explaining how much you get paid from customers is much easier for the potential distributor to understand. This has helped us sponsor more distributors and makes it much easier for new distributors to explain to their prospects how the business works!

Hopefully at this point, we've done our job and "sold" you on the importance of getting customers. We highly recommend that you spend time this week to create your action plan for building a customer base. If you're completely stumped on how to promote your product or service, answer questions, get the person enrolled, or even what to say, then check out our Product Personal Endorsement course. The Product Personal Endorsement course breaks down the entire process of what it takes to get a customer. You'll know exactly what to say when someone asks you about your product or service, and how to introduce it when you know your product or service could help someone. We show the exact methodology we use, from an initial conversation to customer enrollment to becoming a referral machine.

We've seen a 100% success rate in getting customers for distributors who go through the course and create their endorsement. In fact, dozens and dozens of people have used this information to become a Top 25 Customer Enroller in our company.

One of the mantras of the Complete Networker is that customers are the lifeblood of your business. The first step in becoming a Complete Networker is learning how to get customers. We **guarantee** that learning how to get customers will change you and your business — **forever**.

Chapter 2

Learn Communication and Sales with "Business Common Sense" and Sponsoring Becomes Easier

Does the thought of using a "cheesy" script on everyone within three feet send shivers of embarrassment down your spine? We can relate and still remember the icky feelings those unprofessional tactics can cause. Before Chris joined his current company, he was "swimming around" in the B.S. of a previous MLM company. It was horrible. The company he was with was a company that embodied much of the MLM "cheesy" B.S.

Immediately after joining this other company, Chris went to the "big time" upline's house to start building his business. He was actually very excited about working with the "big time" upline, until he learned what he was supposed to do. Chris was told to start dialing the "A's" in his cell phone. When his friends answered the phone, he would say, "I'm working with some extremely successful business people and want to introduce you to them..." Then Chris handed over his phone to his upline. His upline went into a high pressured sales tactic of nailing down a time so he could go "show the plan."

Chris recalls, "I almost vomited on the table from this technique!" However, Chris was determined to "push through his comfort zone" and build the business. Looking back, he wasn't pushing through his comfort zone, but rather his common sense zone! It doesn't take a Ph.D. to guess what happened. Chris got zero sponsorships and zero results (unless you count the friends who made fun of Chris or avoided him as getting results!).

His upline kept telling him, "You have to go through the 'nos' to find the 'yeses' and 'the diamonds in the rough.'" Since Chris's warm market was tapped out, his upline told him it's time to turn to the cold market. Chris was excited because it meant he wouldn't have to embarrass himself with his friends anymore. Talking to strangers would be a piece of cake! Or so he thought.

Cheesy Method #1: Hang out in the business and financial section of the bookstore and wait until a "sharp looking person" came in and picked up a book. Chris was told to then strike up a conversation and set up an appointment in order to show the business presentation.

Cheesy Method #2: Chris was instructed to go out with his upline and use the buddy system to start conversations. One person would strike up a conversation and say, "You see that person over there?" as he pointed to the other one. "He's set to retire in the next two to four years... you have to meet him!" Anyone who wanted to meet the other one was a "hot" prospect and was invited to the weekly opportunity presentation.

Neither of these methods produced any results. To put it bluntly, Chris felt like a complete idiot because of this "cheesy" MLM B.S. At about the same time Chris was "swimming through" his MLM B.S. in his soon to be ex-MLM company, Jason started applying his "business common sense" to his network marketing business. He asked himself, "What would I do if I was still running my law firm?"

Jason imagined himself implementing MLM style sales and communication into the law firm... and started laughing! The obvious jumped out to him that the "cheesy" MLM stuff was so far off what real sales were or what any business would ever use, that it needed to be trashed immediately.

Jason knew a "natural law" about human psychology. And everything that was taught in MLM went against it. The "natural law" is that people love to buy, but hate to be sold to. Do you enjoy it when people knock on your front door and try to sell you something? No! However, we do not know anyone who does not enjoy the buying experience. Who doesn't enjoy going out and selecting something new that they want? It's just human nature.

Once you apply this "natural law" to your business, you'll have more fun and get more results. You'll also lose that icky feeling that is created when you try to convince people to join your business when using the "cheesy" MLM training.

One of the mantras of the Complete Networker is to stop selling and start helping people buy what they want and need. The typical MLM training B.S. is to talk with everyone within three feet and "show the plan, show the plan, and show the plan." The problem with that is that you're basically shoving your business and product down people's throats. No one likes that. Rather than just going through your phone list, as you may have been told to do, learn how a Complete Networker effectively communicates and gains customers and new distributors.

Once Jason had success in his MLM business by applying his "business common sense," he created a five step communication process to teach his team. These five steps are what he also taught Chris in order to help him have success. The communication process has helped us sell tens of millions of dollars' worth of products and services in our MLM business and other businesses. When you consider the people that we've mentored and partnered with who have used this communication process, we're probably into the hundred million dollar range of sales. The rest of this chapter will give you an overview of these five steps.

The Connect Step: Build Relationships

Understand that not everyone is going to need or want your product, service, or the business opportunity. We'll stress that point again: no matter how great your product is or how amazing your compensation plan is, not everyone is going to want or need them. Stop looking at people as "prospects with dollar signs floating over their heads" and, rather, look at them as people. Treat people the way you want to be treated... like a real person! New concept... we know! (Sarcasm added on purpose.) Be "normal" and have a conversation.

You don't have to mention your MLM business or product in every conversation that you have. Manipulative uplines and training courses will tell you to always bring up your company and find the people who are ready to listen. That approach is incredibly short-sighted and very stupid. It's okay to have normal relationships and conversations that don't revolve around MLM. Actually, for the Complete Networker, it's **required that you have normal relationships and conversations.**

Before we continue, we want to stress that we are not just telling you to talk with people, so you can pounce on them with your MLM business once they say something. Having relationships with people is part of being human. Everyone we know lives a more fulfilled life when they have meaningful relationships with people. In our eyes, MLM is a great "excuse" to focus on forming relationships. Besides living a more fulfilled life by building relationships, you get a lot of other great benefits, too. Sponsoring distributors and getting customers are just two of the benefits.

A fun and powerful exercise is to go out and talk with people and not allow yourself to talk about your MLM business! This exercise will force you to focus on building relationships. We've noticed a very interesting trend when people focus on building relationships; they have more fun and have more success in their MLM company.

Now what happens when you ask enough questions and build enough relationships? People will naturally say something that is a perfect lead in for your MLM business opportunity, product, or service:

- "My commute is killing me..."
- "I lose sleep over my shrinking 401(k) plan..."
- "I never get to see my family..."
- "I don't get paid what I'm worth..."

The Develop Step: Build a Bridge

When you hear those phrases, alarms probably start going off in your head; "My MLM company can help this person!" A common mistake distributors make is to immediately jump in and start talking about their company, product, and comp plan. The excitement leads the distributor to blabbing and eventually puking so much information on the person, all they get back is a blank stare and awkward silence in the conversation. Those are no fun!

You have to put yourself in the person's shoes, as they have no idea what you're talking about. You've already made the mental connection that MLM (and your company and product) can help the person achieve his goal or solve his problem. But they haven't made that connection! For example, they may only know about saving money, cutting back on expenses, or getting a second (or third) job to bring in more money. Here you are talking about the world's greatest widget, infinite levels of payout, and getting six people who get six people…

Can you see why the disconnect happens? Are any light bulbs from previous conversations going off? This awkward disconnect is the #1 communication mistake that MLM distributors make. And it's completely avoidable! An incredibly critical step in the Complete Networker's communication process is skipped over. This step is called the Develop step.

The Develop step is what helps a person understand that MLM and your company can help them out. It helps the person "connect the dots" between where they are and where you are. If you skip the Develop step, you are just asking for painful conversations that get no results. Once you learn the Develop step, you'll have people asking you questions and wanting to learn more! Now, all of sudden, the process of sharing your MLM opportunity becomes smooth and fun.

Imagine that your prospect is standing on the edge of the Mississippi River. The solution to his or her problem, your MLM opportunity, is on the other side of the river. When you immediately jump into your company, you're basically kicking your prospect into the river, hoping he or she can swim to the other side. Very few people can swim across and "survive." The Develop step is as though you're building a bridge for the person so he can get across safely. A lot fewer people get swept down river this way. This example is a great visual because it's dramatic and makes you pause before sharing your company's details. You don't want your prospects trying to swim and end up getting swept downriver.

The Develop step is a critical, "must have" step. However, there's not a magic bullet script or phrase that you always say. Just as each bridge is built differently to cross rivers, each bridge that you build with your prospects will be different. They'll have a lot of similarities, but they won't be exactly the same. The best way to really understand the Develop step is to look back and figure out what bridge was built for you. What information, concepts, books, presentations, conversations, and so on, led you to MLM and your company? Spend a few minutes to identify those. You'll probably have a short list compiled.

We both read a popular financial education book that made us have a paradigm shift in regards to producing income and working differently. Jason's paradigm shift was seeing the limitations in the law firm. While it was very successful and brought in over six figures a month, he had to be there to make it successful. For Chris, he was exposed to a world of alternatives other than getting a job to pay the bills and spending three hours a day commuting. After reading this popular book, we were both primed for the MLM industry. The normal MLM presentation of product, comp plan, and leverage now all of a sudden made sense to us. The concepts helped us connect the dots between what MLM is and what it could do for us.

At the time, Chris had no clue about the Develop step. But Jason did. He trained Chris to use various business and finance books to help him build his business. Chris bought multiple copies of each book and started loaning them out to his friends. Some people read the book, some didn't. But those who did read it had the seed planted and were in the mindset of creating financial independence and not relying on a job for income. Can you see how that set up the perfect lead in for MLM and Chris's company?

Quite a few people ended up joining his downline. Here's the really powerful part... the people that Chris developed and gave the book to, but didn't join his downline, now had a seed planted. They knew there were other ways to make money, and they knew that Chris was doing something other than a job. Chris had these conversations back in the 2004-2005 time frame. Since then, many of those people with seeds planted, have come back to Chris asking for information on what he's doing. Even in the year 2013, he still has people calling him to ask questions and get more details. Let that sink in. Most MLMers are taught to go through the "nos" until they find the right person and get a "yes." The Develop step has people from the last decade still thinking about our company and calling us for more details, because their life situation has changed.

How powerful is that?

As you get more experience, you'll have different ways of taking people through the Develop step. It's similar to how a carpenter or mechanic has different tools in his toolbox to get a job done. You'll want to always add more methods for the Develop step to your toolbox. The next chapter will go into more detail on a tool that we created for the Develop step and will give you instructions on how you can use it, too.

This exercise will help you become a Complete Networker by having success with the Develop step and building relationships:

Step #1: Have conversations with people, but no matter what, do **not** mention your MLM or your product.

Step #2: After the conversation, write down a summary of your conversation. Try to identify what you could do with him or her in regards to the Develop step.

Step #3: Sleep on it for a night. Take the best idea that you came up with and write out a response to the person.

Step #4: Next time you talk with the person, implement the Develop step!

Normally, we have our downline discuss what they're going to say and do with us first, so we can help them. Unfortunately, we can't do that with every reader of this book. Doing the exercise will help you start developing this skill and becoming a better communicator.

The Introduce Step: Presenting Your Company

We constantly get asked, "What presentation should I use to present my MLM business?" There is no one perfect presentation to use! In fact, we do not care for the word *presentation* because it gets most people into a mindset of sitting down with the person and doing an hour or longer canned presentation from their company or upline. The problem with canned presentations is that they get the distributor tunnel visioned on the material and getting through it and not on what the prospect is actually interested in. More often than not, the distributor ends up talking and rambling himself out of a new distributor or customer.

We prefer the concept of *introducing* when it comes to showing information on our company and/or product. The Introduce step is about tailoring the information to the person's interest, rather than giving a canned presentation. We ask the person, "There are hours and hours of information that I could go over with you, but that's not going to be productive for either of us. What's important to you? What do you want to learn more about?" Giving people information that they are interested in will dramatically increase the chance of them joining you or becoming a customer. Who wants to sit through a bunch of information that they have no interest in?

It's critical that you understand that what you think is important may not be what your prospect thinks is important. Please don't give information to someone just because it's the standard presentation from your company. For example, MLM distributors love showing the compensation plan, but very few people actually care about the specifics of it! We almost never show or talk about the compensation plan. If someone asks how they make money, we walk them through the customer payout from the previous chapter, not the compensation plan. People, unless they are career network marketers, do not care about the mechanics of the compensation plan. They just want to know what they need to do in order to make money.

Another reason to stop doing formal, hour long presentations is because of the "YouTube effect." YouTube has changed the way many people get information and entertainment. People now want information that they are interested in, when they want it, and in short time segments. The "YouTube effect" is the exact opposite of the canned MLM presentation. Don't fight the trend. Rather, embrace it and you'll sponsor more distributors.

We routinely have conversations about our MLM business with prospects to find out what they are interested in and what questions they have. Rather than spending an hour trying to explain all the information or answer the questions, we send them an email with a few links to pertinent information. The links are typically YouTube videos (either ones we created or that our company did), PDF documents, or particular sections of a website. The email allows the person to review the information when it suits his schedule and leverages our time so we can get more done. We love our company and MLM, but we don't want to spend hours every time someone wants information, repeating the exact information over and over. Rather, we would rather leverage the available resources and our time with the Introduce step.

Replacing your MLM presentation with the Introduce step will take some getting used to, but, it's well worth it. Businesses that fight trends go out of business. People that fight trends get left in the dust. People and businesses that adapt with the trends have success. Learning the Introduce step will get more prospects reviewing your company's information, free up more of your time, and grow your business faster.

The Follow-up Step: The Fortune Really is in the Follow-up

You've probably heard the phrase, "The Fortune is in the Follow-up." The fortune *really* is in the follow-up. Over the years, we've seen many distributors (both in and out of our downline) lose out on new distributors because of poor and improper follow-up. We don't want you to be one of those distributors. There are two main reasons people screw-up the follow-up:

1. They don't know what to do or say.
2. They lose track of people because they are not organized.

This section will discuss the first point of not knowing what to say or do. Chapter 5, *Get Organized!,* will help you with the second point.

After you have introduced information to a person, he is now in the Follow-up step. The purpose of the Follow-up step is to:

1. See if the person reviewed the information. If he didn't, then get him to review it.
2. Answer questions and clarify any points from the information he reviewed.
3. Get him more information, if needed.

Going into much more detail on the Follow-up step is out of the scope of this book because there are many different scenarios and possibilities. However, a story about one of Jason's sponsorships will highlight the importance of the Follow-up step. Jason ended up following-up with this person eight times before he joined Jason's business. This person was a sales professional and said to Jason, "I'm in sales and I'm impressed with the way you contacted me. You were never pushy and seemed to always call at just the right time. Your style made it so I couldn't ignore your calls or voicemails..." This person signed up and turned out to be a "sponsor monster" who sponsored a ton of new distributors. Needless to say, this person helped propel Jason's business. Jason wouldn't have successfully sponsored the person unless he knew what he was doing and how to follow-up.

How many new distributors or sponsor monsters have you missed out on because of poor follow-up?

The Close Step: Get to a Decision Point and Ask for the Sale

Your goal is to get every person to a decision point. Notice, we said decision point and not a new distributor or new customer. You cannot realistically expect to sign up every person you talk with. It's a great thought, but it's not going to happen. We want you to focus on getting everyone to a decision point. A "Yes, I'm signing up" or "No, I'm not signing up" answer. If you're getting people to a decision point, it means you're doing the communication process correctly. If you're successful at getting people to a decision point, then you will recruit new distributors and acquire new customers.

A common mistake by MLM distributors is that they never ask the person if he wants to sign up. You have to ask for the sale! However, many distributors have trouble asking the people to join as a distributor or become a customer. Some have trouble because they lack self-confidence. Some have trouble because they have "money issues." Over the years, we've heard many reasons why. They almost all boil down to a belief issue in the person's head. While, this book cannot play the role of therapist, it can still help you.

The easiest way to overcome your obstacle is by just asking the person, "Are you ready to get started?" Asking a direct question often makes MLM distributors uncomfortable. The reality is that if you want to build a successful MLM organization, you need to learn the Close step and how to be direct with people. Once you ask the question, you need to remain silent until the other person talks. No exceptions! We've witnessed too many distributors talk themselves out of sales. Just ask the question and zip your lips. Do not talk until the other person does, even if it feels like an eternity of silence.

The person will either say "yes" or "no." If he says "yes," then congratulations! If he says "no," then ask, "Why not?" and stay silent. This direct line of questioning is how you get people to a decision point and into your downline. People will tell you what concerns are holding them back or what additional questions they have. This process will lead the prospect to a decision point where he either joins or does not join. Sometimes, you'll realize this is a person you do not want to work with because he never makes a decision and just keeps wasting your time.

Answering Questions and Objections

Questions and objections can come up anywhere in the communication process, but you'll get the most in the Follow-up and Close step. Don't be afraid of questions or objections because they are actually a good sign! It shows that the person is engaged in what you're sharing and is thinking about the information. Be happy when people ask you questions.

You need to be prepared when people ask questions. Memorizing "cheesy" answers does not count as being prepared. They will do more harm than good. Below is a six step process to help you with answering questions and addressing objections.

1. **Listen** - Completely listen to the person and let them finish their thoughts. Do not interrupt and assume you know the answer!

2. **Pause** - Once the person has finished asking the question - PAUSE for a few seconds. Often times the person will want to fill the "void of silence" and continue speaking, giving you his real question or objection.

3. **Clarify** - Make sure you understand what the person is really asking. Often times he says one thing, but you hear something else. Ask additional questions to clarify before answering. Clarify, clarify, and clarify!

4. **Answer** - After you have listened, paused, and clarified, then answer the question. Do not use "cheesy & quick" scripts. Do your best to relate the answer to a point of reference with which the person is familiar.

5. **Confirm** - Confirm with the person that you answered the question to his or her satisfaction. You can usually tell by body language, tone, or his response. Don't move on until they are "over the speed bump."

6. **Next Step** - Once you've answered the question, it's your job to keep the conversation moving forward. Resume the conversation or move on to the next step.

Personality Types

Identifying and understanding personality types will not only help you tremendously in MLM, but also other areas of your life. It's almost as though you will have a crystal ball in understanding how people will make decisions, how much information they need or want, and their own behaviors. Understanding personality types will help you become a better communicator because you'll be able to give the person the information the way he wants it.

A person's preference for information often comes down to his personality type. Some people need to review all the information from beginning to end before they can make decision. Other people just want the bullet points and ask you a few questions. One way is not better than the other way. It's just how people are wired. You need to make sure you're giving the amount and type of information to the right personality type! If you give too many details to someone who doesn't want details, you will overwhelm him and he will never go through with it.

Detailing the different personality types and how they relate to the communication process is out of the scope of this book. We did want to briefly touch on them so you are aware of them and can keep them in mind as you talk with people.

Improving Your Communication Skills

Hopefully the overview on our communication process has given you insight into how you can improve. Or, if you've been fed a bunch of "cheesy" MLM training, it's given you hope that you can run your business in a professional way that will make you feel proud.

If you want more help on becoming a Complete Networker in regards to communication, then go through our Communication Course. It goes into a tremendous amount of detail on each step of the communication process, personality types, and answering questions. It's tailored to help people in the MLM industry get results by using a "business common sense" communication and sales approach.

Chapter 3

A Simple and Effective Marketing Funnel to Help You Recruit Distributors

Becoming proficient in the Communication Steps outlined in the last chapter can take some time. Mastering the Communication Steps can take much longer. The time required is why you need a simple, yet effective, marketing funnel for new distributors in your organization to learn and use. Having your new distributors constantly falling on their faces with minimal success is not good for them or your MLM organization. A simple and effective marketing funnel helps your new distributors have immediate success, while they are learning and mastering the Communication Steps.

Creating a simple and effective marketing funnel is challenging and very few MLM organizations have one. We debated whether or not to even use the phrase "marketing funnel," not because what we're about to show you isn't a marketing funnel, rather because there is typically a lot of hype associated with the phrase. Almost on a daily basis we see ads and Facebook posts with outrageous claims, such as, "You'll recruit 30 new distributors in the next seven days with this ultimate marketing funnel that will have prospects begging you to join your MLM opportunity with credit card in hand!" We're sure you've seen those ads and webinars. They are just more of the typical "cheesy" MLM B.S. We don't want anything we create associated with nonsense such as that.

It's important to understand that a marketing funnel is just a series of steps that a potential distributor or customer goes through. A step can be many things, such as, watching videos, having a conversation, reviewing a website, or participating in a three-way call or meeting. Having a well defined marketing funnel helps out in different ways:

- It makes building the business much easier for new distributors because there is a "1-2-3" step process to follow.
- It leverages distributors' time effectively because rather than having to spend time explaining every detail to every prospect, a marketing step can do that. A distributor could have dozens or even hundreds of prospects going through the marketing funnel simultaneously.
- It allows distributors to effectively utilize the knowledge and success of someone else.

We could go into much detail in describing the benefits of marketing funnels, but we're not going to because there is a tremendous amount of free information available on the Internet. Besides, you're probably more interested in getting results! Just understand that there is no "magic bullet" marketing funnel that will build the business for you. Please block and ignore the constant stream of "Ultimate Marketing Funnel" B.S.

Rather than trying to write about how to create a marketing funnel, we're going to share the one that we currently use in our own MLM organization. Our marketing funnel is not going to recruit 30 new distributors within the next seven days of reading about it. Nope! But, it will help you work toward recruiting the type of person who is committed to becoming a long term distributor who is willing to put in work for delayed gratification. Before we share the marketing funnel with you, we need to give you some background information.

The Anti Suit Entrepreneur

Building a solid MLM organization has allowed us to create an amazing life. We live where we want to, get up when we want to, work when we want to, pursue new business and investing ideas, and tackle projects that are important to us. We've been living this lifestyle since 2005. Many people want the lifestyle that we have. Needless to say, we've had hundreds, if not thousands, of people ask over the years, "How are you able to live that lifestyle? Can you show me how I can, too?" Getting those questions is every MLM distributors dream come true! We get those questions, but our new downline distributors do not.

To answer those questions and to help distributors, we wrote and published a book titled the *Anti Suit Entrepreneur: Live Life on Your Terms, Escape the Suit & Tie and Learn New Rules for the Economy*. It doesn't mention MLM or our company directly. However, the book describes how we are able to live the life that we do, while giving practical tips and information to the reader on how he can start living life on his terms. The book is designed to get the reader thinking entrepreneurially and about how he can take care of himself financially, without relying on a job. The book will also help the person avoid many of the common mistakes that new entrepreneurs make.

We wanted it to be more than just another book that people read. We also created a website, www.AntiSuitEntrepreneur.com, and an online community for entrepreneurs. We did this because many business and entrepreneur books leave the reader wondering at the end of the book, "This book was nice and everything… but what am I supposed to do next?" We wanted to provide a solution to the person and help him start his entrepreneurial journey. Learning the entrepreneurial mindset using the MLM model has changed our lives. We want to help other people do the same.

The Three Steps to Success Marketing Funnel

We call our simple and effective marketing funnel the *Three Steps to Success.* We'll give you a brief overview in this section and then instructions so you can see the entire process yourself, just as a potential MLM distributor would. It's important to understand that while the book has great information, a person does **not** need to read it in order to go through the funnel and partner with you in your MLM company. The book is referenced throughout the marketing funnel to lend credibility to the information. The marketing funnel is done entirely through the website of www.AntiSuitEntrepreneur.com. This allows people the convenience to access it 24/7 from anywhere on any device (computer, tablet, or phone).

It's not practical for us to describe each step in detail because they change. We're constantly testing and improving the funnel to help people get better results. This funnel is used with online lead generation, as well as people's personal networks. Most people have thought about starting businesses and becoming entrepreneurs, but few have acted on that desire. Our marketing funnel is designed to get people thinking about their finances, life, and entrepreneurial goals. It will also help them get into "action mode" and start a business. It's a powerful tool that will help you with the Develop step.

We discuss how MLM is where we got our entrepreneurial start and how MLM has allowed us to live life on our terms. It does **not** mention a specific company or product. Since we introduce MLM with our credibility and the Anti Suit Entrepreneur concepts, we minimize almost all objections that often surround MLM.

While we are big proponents of the MLM industry, we don't shove it down people's throats. There are different ways people can achieve living life on their terms. Generally speaking, MLM is the best vehicle for helping people start their entrepreneurial journey. Without the skills and residual income we gained from MLM, we would not have been able to start other successful businesses. New distributors should set up a three-way call or meeting with their upline to help with introducing the MLM company and product or service. More experienced distributors, who have become proficient in the Communication Steps, can do it on their own.

This marketing funnel sets you up perfectly to introduce the details of your MLM company and how it can help the person live the Anti Suit Entrepreneur lifestyle. The Anti Suit Entrepreneur lifestyle is an extremely desirable one that many people want. The way the Anti Suit Entrepreneur lifestyle is presented is often more desirable than the MLM lifestyle. Typically, the MLM lifestyle is presented as driving around in flashy cars, living in big houses, and having expensive jewelry. The Anti Suit Entrepreneur lifestyle focuses on the person living life on his terms and doing what he wants. Guess which one resonates more with the person? More people want to do what's important to them, rather than drive a Ferrari.

Let's be honest with the current environment of MLM: there's too much hype and "get rich quick" mentality. Whether through previous MLM experiences or an Internet based business, most people have been burned before and are fatigued from the constant bombardment of hype. The *Three Steps to Success* marketing funnel is refreshingly different from other marketing funnels and MLM business presentations because it doesn't have any hype. In fact, it's quite the opposite! The concepts are presented in a very matter-of-fact manner to educate the person. It also tells people that it's going to take time, effort, money, and short term sacrifice in order to build a business that supports the Anti Suit Entrepreneur lifestyle. People go to college for four or more years for a degree. Most businesses take two to five years to become profitable. Building an MLM business, especially part time, is no different. It takes time, typically two to five years. We tell people that up front. Guess what? Most people love it that we're direct and honest. They tell us our no-nonsense approach is refreshing.

Will the *Three Steps to Success* marketing funnel recruit every person for you? No, of course not. But the people who resonate with the Anti Suit Entrepreneur message are the people you want in your organization. They are the high quality and long term people. They are willing to commit time, money, and effort to build the business. They are willing to work hard for delayed gratification. They are the people who will help you build a solid MLM organization.

Go Through the Three Steps Yourself

The brief overview almost makes the *Three Steps to Success* marketing funnel sound too simple. It's not. It's very simple to understand and for the prospect to go through. However, our system that manages the marketing funnel is doing complex tracking and contact management for you. No matter where the person is in the process, the system tracks it and records it. This allows you to see exactly what the prospect viewed and for how long. It's helpful to know if the person viewed 30 seconds or 3 minutes or 30 minutes of a video! In a nutshell, it's a system we built from the ground up to support the network marketing business model. Future chapters will discuss the details of this system.

The *Three Steps to Success* marketing funnel is the most effective, when it comes to simple "1-2-3" marketing funnels, in taking someone through the Develop Step and building a bridge to MLM, as discussed in the previous chapter. Depending on how experienced the distributor is and the prospect with whom he is talking, the funnel is flexible and can be changed. As we wrote earlier, it's much easier for you to understand when you go through the process yourself. You can go through it by creating a free account at www.MLMCompletePackage.com/CompleteNetworker/FreeAccount. To be clear, a free account will grant you access so you can view the marketing funnel yourself. If you decide you want to use it to help build your business, you'll have to upgrade to a paid account.

The free account will also allow you to download the Anti Suit Entrepreneur Marketing Method. A Marketing Method is a training document written to explain a given marketing funnel in detail and all the different ways it can be used. The Anti Suit Entrepreneur Marketing Method will go into all the details of how you can use the *Three Steps to Success* marketing funnel and other available resources to help build your business. It's a free download that you can access after you create your free account. The words from an MLM distributor sum everything up nicely: "Wow, I was excited about this book, but after reading the Marketing Method, I had no idea how powerful this was. This is more than a book. It's a complete marketing plan!"

While you don't need to read the book in order to use the Marketing Method and the *Three Steps to Success* marketing funnel, we still recommend that you do. It'll not only give you the complete picture on what an Anti Suit Entrepreneur is, but hopefully give you some more practical "business common sense" building tips. If want to read the *Anti Suit Entrepreneur* book, go to http://www.AntiSuitEntrepreneur.com/GetIt

Whether you use our marketing funnel or not, you need to have one for your team. Following the typical MLM marketing funnel of "make a list of everyone you know, get excited, tell them to watch a video on the website, and then present the business" isn't going to cut it. You may be able to make that work, but the vast majority of the distributors you recruit will not. Creating duplication in your MLM organization is a necessity in order to build a long term MLM business.

Chapter 4

Duplicate and Train with "Business Common Sense"

While running the law firm, Jason knew how important well trained employees and staff were to the firm's success and profitability. Since the firm had to pay them a salary starting the first day of their job, he wanted to make sure they were as effective as possible in their jobs as quickly as possible. The better they were at their jobs, the more clients and cases the law firm could take on. More cases and clients equaled more revenue and greater profit. Jason was very good at bringing in new clients and increasing revenue. He opened two new law offices in just a few years. A large part of his success was because he was very methodical in how he trained his employees.

When Jason joined his network marketing company, he knew that there was a difference between hiring employees and training MLM Distributors. So he joined with a humble attitude and was ready to learn. Again, he was in for another shock at the manipulative MLM B.S. that distributors (even distributors in his upline) pulled! It was the mentality of "Go out there and sponsor people. And then when you do sponsor someone tell him to go sponsor people. But most importantly keep your attention and focus on sponsoring more people... you must lead by example and sponsor, sponsor, and sponsor!"

That was the summary of the training that Jason received from his upline. It was pretty much the WHOLE training manual for the team. It didn't take long for his "business common sense" to kick in and say, "This makes absolutely no freaking sense! No business, MLM or not, can be successful this way!" Uplines and gurus pull this manipulative B.S. because they have no idea how to train a distributor in their downline. Rather than admit they can't train, they just tell people to go out and sponsor!

There are a few possible outcomes to this stupid and ineffective way of building.

Outcome #1: Distributors Mentally Self Destruct

This is probably the most common outcome. After going through the so called "training," distributors have a voice of doubt in the back of their mind. This voice is saying, "What happens when I do sponsor someone? How will I train them? I don't even know what I'm doing!" Now the distributors may never share this thought with anyone. They may try to ignore it themselves because they want to build. But the seed of doubt is planted and it will just grow.

We've seen countless distributors with prospects who are **ready to sign up, but the distributors are terrified to sponsor them**! And they actually won't sponsor the prospects because of that "seed of doubt!" The MLM distributors lack confidence and faith in their ability to help get the new person trained. No matter how good the company or product is, this lack of confidence will stop many distributors from sponsoring new people. It took us years to pinpoint this issue. We now firmly believe this is the number one reason distributors don't sponsor people into their downline.

Outcome #2: Treadmill Syndrome Sets In

Some of those people get past the "seed of doubt" (or don't develop it until later) and are able to sponsor some distributors with their initial excitement, goals they set, and a "get it done" attitude. Life is usually good for a couple of months. They are getting commission checks, making small rank advancements, and receiving recognition from their upline and company! But, then distributors they sponsored start quitting. "Well, that's fine... MLM isn't for everyone... I'll just sponsor some more people."

After this happens a few times, the **Treadmill Syndrome** starts settling in. The Treadmill Syndrome is where people start falling off as fast as you're sponsoring. Building your business eventually becomes like running on a treadmill--you're building and sponsoring but your business isn't really getting anywhere! Eventually most distributors get burned out and quit. You can only run on the treadmill so long before you need to get off.

Outcome #3: A Trail of Carnage

This "sponsor, sponsor, and sponsor more" mentality can lead to success, if a distributor does sponsor enough people. He or she will get a couple of other people who can do the same. However, it leaves a **Trail of Carnage**. To find those couple of people, you'll need to sponsor hundreds (even thousands) of distributors along the way. That leaves a lot of unhappy distributors who join the business and then quit. Hence the label, Trail of Carnage.

This is a very shortsighted way of building the business because what happens to those thousands of distributors who joined and quit? They had a bad experience and will go around and let anyone who will listen know about their experience! That negativity doesn't help the long term growth of the business, the company as a whole, or the MLM industry. Most people can't do this method because after just a little bit of carnage, they feel guilty for not truly being able to help their downline.

You also need a **secret lead source or method** for sponsoring all those people. For example, Jason's upline had such a secret lead source. His upline was working directly with a very popular financial author at the time who used his name to generate massive amounts of leads. A handful of people (Jason's upline being one of them) were gravy trained with these leads. It was NOT duplicatable and only a handful of people could really benefit from it. It left a lot of carnage along the way. Once the popular financial author was no longer popular and they lost their secret lead source, they started retiring or moving onto other companies...because they truly couldn't build the business!

Jason realized all of this as he applied his "business common sense" and broke away from his upline and worked completely on his own. He was determined to have a truly duplicatable way for his entire team to build their businesses. We won't take you through all the details of how he figured it out... but fast forward a couple of years from when he broke away from his upline:

- Jason built an international business and a full-time income.
- Jason figured things out and taught and helped Chris build a full time income within three and half years.
- Thousands of distributors in Jason's company, but outside his downline, started subscribing to Jason's training and marketing system to learn the techniques.

The rest of this chapter will focus on what you need to know so you can train your downline.

Don't Overcomplicate It!

Remember, building an MLM business is made up of three areas: getting customers, sponsoring distributors, and training your team. That's the essence of building a solid MLM business. So, don't get caught up in all these fancy courses or personal development seminars that cost thousands or even tens of thousands of dollars to help you "have a break through" to figure out what's holding you back.

Training your team is as simple as teaching them how to get customers, sponsor distributors, and do the same with their team. Those three areas seem so simple that many people overlook them. They think, "It can't be that easy to build the business..." Memorize the three areas so when you get confused or off track down the road, you can refer back to the basics and what works.

Can You Get Customers?

This is a "yes" or "no" answer. Either you can get customers or you cannot. If you can't say "yes" to that question now, then take our Communication Course and our Customer Personal Endorsement course, so you can say "yes." You might be wondering, "What does my getting customers have to do with training my team?" It's simple. If you can't get customers, you won't be able to teach your team to get customers. We've seen people who don't actually get customers, just tell their team to go through a course so they can get customers. The "do as I say, not as I do" doesn't work.

Can You Sponsor a Distributor?

Again, this is a "yes" or "no" answer. If you have someone to train your team, then it means that "yes" you can sponsor someone. If your answer is "no," then go through our Communication Training and the Business Personal Endorsement to get help. You're probably thinking, "Well, just because I can sponsor someone, doesn't mean that I can teach someone else how to..."

That thought brings us to the next point: You're not 100% responsible for the success of your team. Note that we said you're not 100% responsible. You're responsible to the point of providing support, guidance, and training resources to your team. At the end of the day, you can't make your downline get a customer.

Even with all of our training, knowledge, and resources, we still have people who join our downline and never take action to build their business. We'll do what we can to help the person and troubleshoot any problems, but we can't make the person build the business (despite how much we want to and know they would kick ass in the business!) We're stressing this point because we know many distributors carry the "weight of the world" on their shoulders when it comes to their team having success. You can't carry all that weight; it'll only drag you down.

You Need a True System In Place for Training.

Notice that we said "true" system. MLM Companies and leaders will talk about their system that they use. Often they're referring to their starter kit that boils down to a checklist, some "You can do it!" motivational CD's, and a replicated website. That's not a system or real training.

A "true" system teaches people exactly what they need to know in order to get results. The best way to think of this is the Basic Training that the U.S. Army takes all of its enlisted soldiers through. In 10 weeks, the U.S. Army can take any person with no knowledge or skills and turn them into a soldier. The new soldier is now able to operate within the Army as a whole. The U.S. Army is the finest example of "duplication in action." The Drill Sergeants, who run Basic Training, have all been through Basic Training themselves!

Jason had a very methodical process that he took his new employees through at the law firm.. That's one of the main reasons he was able to expand the business. Putting the Basic Training and new employee orientation concept into perspective, why wouldn't you do that with your MLM business? Why don't you have a complete step by step training to take all of your people through? We asked ourselves those same questions. That's one of the reasons we created the Complete Networker, various training courses, and marketing system at MLMCompletePackage.com

We originally created them to train our own downline. As our businesses grew, we simply didn't have enough time to teach all of the material. So we "systematized" everything to leverage our time and knowledge, but to also ensure that our downlines' downlines' downlines were following the exact same steps that we were.

If you don't have a "true" system in place, then things will get lost in translation. It's happened in our downline when people didn't get their team plugged into our Boot Camp training. We've had people way down in our downline come to us and say, "I don't know how to build the business...." We then find out that their sponsor didn't get them plugged into our Boot Camp training! Well, once we got the distributor plugged in and started on the Boot Camp, they felt confident in their ability to build the business. Problem solved!

Using a "true" system won't train your team 100% on autopilot. That's just impossible. Network marketing is a people business. A "true" system can help your team get 90% there. It'll teach the necessary basics and core skills. This method takes the pressure of "knowing everything" off of you and frees up a lot of your time. The other 10% will come from asking their sponsor questions or attending weekly training calls. A "true" system is what will allow you to build your business part time, stay focused on "money making activities," and truly train your team so they have everything they need for success.

"But, Chris and Jason, I don't have a 'true' system. What do I do?" That's exactly why we created MLMCompletePackage.com. Over the years, while we had our training and marketing system for our downline and other distributors in our company, we had hundreds of people outside of our system wanting to plug in. Some people were so desperate for good training and a 'true' system that they actually used our training, even though it referenced our company and product directly... and they got results in their business! We created MLMCompletePackage.com to fill that need for people. To be clear, all of the training courses and information on the site are non-company specific, so you and other distributors from other companies can use it to build your business. The training courses and marketing system that you have access to at MLMCompletePackage.com is the **exact same that our downline uses.**

It's our experience that the vast majority of MLM "gurus" create and sell products so they can make a profit. They make their living not from MLM, but from the tools business. We've even met quite a few who don't even have an MLM organization left! Yet, they're still selling tools teaching how to build the business. All of our training courses come from a training need that we have in our downline. We create the courses, so we can make money with our MLM business by helping our downline get more customers and sponsor more distributors.

Our business is building our MLM Residual Income... not being an MLM 'Guru.'

The training courses at MLMCompletePackage represent about 95% of all the training that we give our own team. The other 5%, which is only on our separate team website, is focused on our company and products. Our training courses will work for you and your business because the skills and knowledge needed to build a successful MLM carry across all network marketing companies and businesses outside of MLM. Below is an example of how you can use MLMCompletePackage to train your team in getting customers. This is the same process that we take our downline through.

Helping Your Team Get Customers

1) Have your distributor go through the Communication Course and the Customer Personal Endorsement Course.
2) While your distributor is going through the course, he'll be writing down questions and doing the exercises.
3) Once the courses are completed, have your distributor email you his Customer Personal Endorsement script.
4) You review it, provide feedback, and send it back.
5) When the endorsement script is ready to go, role play with your downline. You act like a prospect and your downline uses his or her endorsement on you. This process may take 15 minutes or a few 30 minute practice sessions. It's well worth it! This practice helps them get ready for the real world.
6) Set a goal for how many times your distributor will use his endorsement in the next week. Tip: From experience, we find 10 to 15 times per week is a good amount to

shoot for. It's not overwhelming to the new person, but it's enough to start growth.

7) Work with your distributor to answer questions or issues as he talks with people. His prospects will ask questions that stump him. Work with your downline to get that figured out. It's "on the job" training!

8) Have your downline keep using his endorsement script until he reaches his goal for customers.

It's that simple.

And this process has a bonus. While you taught your downline how to get a customer, you also taught him how to train his future distributors! You just took him through the process that he'll take his team through. Pretty cool, huh? This process works because you, and everyone else, are referencing the same training courses. Having everyone in your team go through the same training courses is the equivalent of the U.S. Army making all of its soldiers go through Basic Training.

This uniformity creates a standard that everyone uses. Nothing will get lost in translation as your downline grows. This will ensure true duplication in your downline. **To have the true "walk away" MLM residual income, your team has to be self-sufficient once you "walk away."** Otherwise your team (and income) will fall apart. We've seen quite a few distributors who tried to "walk away" from their businesses to retire, and their businesses and income fell apart. Many of those people ended up going back to Corporate America to get a job because they didn't have the heart to start over. It's very sad to see. But it's also very easy to prevent if you're using a "true" system.

What's the best "true" system for you and your MLM organization? Ultimately, it's the one that helps you and your team get results. Our "true" system is available to anyone in the MLM industry at www.MLMCompletePackage.com. If you end up creating your own system or seek out different ones, just make sure you don't get caught up in hype and over complicate the training. There are countless systems and training programs that promise to put your business on autopilot and generate endless leads for you. We haven't used or tried all the available systems, but the ones we have used fall far short of their promises. No system or training can put your business on autopilot. If the claims sound too good to be true, then they probably are. Avoid the hype and make sure you stay focused on providing your team training on getting customers, recruiting distributors, and training new team members.

Chapter 5

How To Really Generate
Leads - Online and Offline!

How often have you said to yourself, "If I only had enough people to talk with each day, I could build a HUGE business. I just need leads!" Every Network Marketer has thought this, including us. At the end of the day, if you don't have people to talk with, you can't build a strong MLM business. Since the Internet became an integral part of our day to day lives, everyone wants the magical source for great quality leads to talk with. And understandably so!

Distributors' needs for leads are why there are so many lead vendors and attraction marketing systems that promise to "generate you hundreds of free leads a week all on autopilot" B.S. The owners of these companies know that the need for leads

61

in MLM is a very easy and profitable emotion to play on. It's that same old manipulative B.S.

Every MLM distributor needs people to talk with in order to build his business. Since we figured out how to generate leads and teach our team to do so, generating leads has been one of the biggest factors for our success. This chapter will focus on the "do's and don'ts" of what you need to know to generate leads without the manipulative B.S.

Don't Buy Leads From a Lead Vendor — No Matter What!

Most people's first thought is to go out and purchase leads from a lead company. Not only is purchasing leads a waste of time and money, but they may actually destroy your downline, too. Over our MLM careers, we've worked with just about every big lead company. We even know a couple of the owners on a personal level. There are a lot of behind-the-scenes things that you, the average MLMer, don't know about. Years ago, generic leads were actually worth the money. But not anymore.

Issue #1: Co-Reg

Have you ever called a purchased lead and the person has no idea who you are and doesn't even remember requesting information? Now believe it or not, there are actually some lead vendors that have people put in names from the phone book, but that's very rare.

Most purchased leads come from co-reg or co-registration. Co-reg is when a person is registering or signing up for something online and they also register for other things at the same time. As the person is registering, he is required to check three to five boxes of other areas of interest (everything from automobiles to Yoga) BEFORE he can move onto the next page. Guess what some of the boxes say? Yep, "Work from home" is on there (or "make money from home," etc). So without even realizing it, the person who was registering for a free account or chance to win a free iPad is now a "hot home based business lead."

Now do you see why often times they have no idea who you are when you call?

Issue #2: Misleading Capture Pages

You go through the numbers and make the dials and finally get a person who did request information. But he is not looking for a business or entrepreneurial opportunity, let alone something he has to spend money on to start! Rather he wants to work from home doing data entry or stuffing envelopes.

That's not the type of person that you're going to build a thriving MLM business on, is it? Not all the leads come from co-reg. Some leads actually opt into a page about working from home. But often it's a misleading page to both you and the prospect. It's all about how it's marketed and what people *want* to see. Lead companies know that people will see what they want to see. Many prospects see work from home as a job to get paid an hourly wage. While MLM distributors will see it as a business opportunity that requires an investment.

Issue #3: Overcalled Leads

You ever have a lead answer the phone to only yell at you that you're the fifth or 15th person to call? There are a few people who do put their information in 10 different forms online, but that's pretty rare (despite what the lead company tells you). Really, what causes this is pretty interesting. There are really only a few real lead vendors in the entire industry that actually generate the leads themselves. The vast majority of companies are resellers or affiliates of the real lead vendors. Typically one of the real lead vendors will only sell its leads two or three times. Selling a lead that many times is reasonable, but once they sell the lead to a reseller or affiliate, they no longer have control over that lead. The reseller will often sell that lead a couple of times and sometimes even to another reseller!

You can probably see how easily it can mushroom from two or three people into 15 or 20. When you call to complain everyone acts like they don't know what is going on because they only sold it to one or two other people. So you're left with an overcalled lead who now blames you.

Issue #4: Rent or Own?

Did you know that you don't actually own a lead you purchase? You're just merely renting their contact details for 30 days. Seriously, go read the fine print in the terms and conditions with your lead vendor. Technically what that means is that you cannot add them to your auto responder (actual CAN-SPAM Act rules - the Internet rules for email marketing) or contact them past the 30 day period. Nuts! Right?

Need we say more about how this is another strike against the lead companies?

Issue #5: Leads Are Not Targeted

Now there are actually a couple of good leads from lead companies. The problem is that once you talk with someone, you need to be on your "A game" because the lead is not targeted to you. While you're calling and talking with the person, so are two or three (or more) other people.

What separates you from the other people calling them? Not much. How good are your phone skills? Usually by the time you get through to a good lead, you're tired and burnt out from dialing 77 unqualified leads! So when the good one answers, you're not exactly on your "A game." Since the lead is not targeted to you and your business, there is nothing to differentiate you from everyone else calling them. When it comes to online marketing and building your business online, you want the leads targeted to you so they know who you are when you call.

Issue #6: Do Lead Companies Really Care About the Quality?

What business are lead companies in? They are in the lead generation business, not in the business of building an MLM organization. How much do they really care about creating high quality leads who are looking for a business? Just enough to make sure MLM distributors come back and buy the leads. Since the lead vendors are not building a downline, they don't really have a vested interest in producing really high quality leads. It's not their downline that is calling the leads.

Issue #7: Don't Destroy Your Downline

If calling generic leads is all you offer your team members and future team members, very few people will survive, let alone have success. You know what we're saying is true. How many leads have you talked with that are just horrible quality and you feel like you're wasting your time with. HINT: Your downline will feel the same way.

When you actually sponsor someone from the generic lead source, you probably had to do a little bit of convincing and then everything from there is an uphill battle. You then have to convince him to buy training materials, to stay on autoship, and try to change his mindset into an entrepreneurial one. Kind of like trying to fit a square peg into a round hole, huh?

At this point, many MLM distributors either grow frustrated and quit or realize they need to take control. To build a large MLM organization, you need to take control of your own marketing and lead generation. You need to learn lead generation. That's about the only way you can guarantee that you'll generate high quality leads.

Don't Use an Attraction Marketing Affiliate Lead Generation System

As MLM distributors determine they need to start taking control and generating their own leads, they inevitably come across attracting marketing systems that offer the ability to earn affiliate income. These systems sound great. However, we've seen way more negative results than positive results when people use these systems. Our advice is to steer clear of these systems, no matter how good they sound. The following story will explain why.

"The Tale of Three Network Marketers"

The actual names of the systems are not used for legal reasons and the names of networkers are not used for privacy reasons.

Network Marketer #1 has been earning a full time MLM multiple six figure income with one company for a number of years. He had a well established income with team members all across the globe. He joined and started promoting one of these online affiliate MLM systems that have you set up a blog and promote yourself as an MLM online marketing guru, even if you have zero experience or success. The ads and sales pages said all the right things to pull him in. He immediately started promoting the system to people in his downline.

As far as we know, he never sponsored any of the leads that came through his website. However, he was very quick to brag about how much affiliate commission he was making off of his downline buying courses, seminars, and system access. We're not talking about a few bucks, we are talking about thousands of dollars in affiliate income from *each* of his downline! There weren't full time leaders in his downline, they were people making a few hundred dollars a month. He had them spending and racking up credit card debt of thousands of dollars. We thought it was stupid and not right to be basically ripping off his downline. And we told him so.

Out of all the downline members who joined the system, zero were using it six months later. Guess what happened to most of those team members? They not only quit the system, but they also quit their MLM business and his downline because they were mad at him. Does that sound like a good system to you?

Here's the kicker.... Networker #1 actually left the online system he was using that helped him go from an MLM newbie to a top income earner. Why? We're not sure, but it's probably because this new affiliate MLM system looked sexy with a lot of hype attached to it. The original system he was using wasn't full of hype, but it got results. Do you want results or do you want hype?

Many people get sucked in by the hype of many of these online systems and programs. Please make sure that you do not. As a side note for leadership training: **NEVER introduce a new system or product or new anything to your team until you have tested it out and had some success with it on your own**. That includes us. We need to earn your trust before you share our training with your team.

Network Marketer #2 is another person we know who had built a solid six figure residual income with his company, mostly through his warm market. He got to the point where he wanted to branch out into online marketing. He joined a very popular system that promises to make you "13 streams of income while you build your primary MLM business." This leader was smart, as he did not introduce this system to his team. He wanted to test it out and see if it actually worked for building his MLM business.

He did everything the system said and put money into marketing and after a couple of months had generated around 70 leads who purchased the same system. That roughly totaled about $700/mo in affiliate income from the system. On the surface that looks pretty good. The idea with this system was to build relationships with those leads and eventually recruit them over to your company. Here are the results:

- Zero signed up as distributors in his company.

- A few months later almost all but a handful of those people quit the system.
- All people he talked with all got sidetracked from building their MLM business and wanted to become affiliate marketers.

After all that work and money invested, he has nothing to show for it in his actual MLM organization, which is what he wanted to build in the first place. Really make sure you understand what happened here: after months of work, he had *nothing* to show for his business and all the MLMer's that he got into the system *stopped* building their own MLM business. You see a problem with this?

The $700/mo he was making quickly trickled down to zero. We have no issue with affiliate income, but it's not nearly as long lasting as a residual income from a well built network marketing business. Affiliate income is just not the same as MLM residual income.

Network Marketer #3 is a relatively new person into the MLM industry. He had no downline or organization built. He went full speed ahead with one of these affiliate lead generation systems. In fact, it was the same system that network marketing #1 from above used. Network marketer #3 *was* one of the people in his downline. He did exactly what the system instructed him to do and he created a website that represented himself as a MLM online marketing guru, even though he had accomplished nothing. Talk about faking it til you make it!

He spent the next year changing his website, buying course after course, flying across the country to attend a conference (that just ended up selling more courses), and making ridiculous YouTube videos (You've seen the silly YouTube videos that many people make.) He told us he spent around $15,000 on all this stuff. After $15,000 and one year, he recruited one person. Yes, only one distributor!

During that year he was also working full time at building his MLM business. He wasn't making a full time income, but rather he had been laid off from his job and decided to work his MLM business full time. He was spending his unemployment money and withdrawing money (and paying the early withdraw penalty) from his 401(k) to fund everything. The whole situation was a train wreck. Not surprisingly, he ended up quitting his MLM company.

Do What a Traditional Business Would Do: Let People Know You're in Business

Remember the mantra of a Complete Networker, "What would a business person with 'business common sense' do?" Jason asked himself that same question. Jason understood that as a business owner, you must market your business through every available channel. When he ran the law firm, he bought radio advertising, the back cover of the Yellow Pages, other local advertising and networked extensively. Yet, one of the most successful ways the law firm got new clients was through networking and referrals from clients! That's why he never understood the "gurus" and systems that said, "Don't waste your time talking with your warm market."

Why the hell would a business owner not let his friends, family, and acquaintances know what his business was? A smart business owner would never do that! Actually, it is quite the opposite. Business owners always have business cards on them and are more than happy to let people know about their businesses. Notice we said *let people know they are in business* not *constantly hound people*. A major problem in the MLM industry is that "cheesy" training has caused distributors to hound people to join the business or buy the products.

Some "cheesy" training teaches the concept of "hound people until they join or die." We paraphrased the trainings because they don't use the words *hound* or *die*, but that's essentially what's being said. It gets distributors convinced that MLM and their business is "right for everyone, it's just a matter of timing. You need to keep talking about it so when the person's situation changes, you're there!" When you stop and think about this, is it really any surprise as to why some people run the other direction when they hear it's MLM?

Do not *hound* people, rather let people know that you're in business. You let people know you're in business by stating it as a fact, just as you do when you describe your job, where you live, what college you went to, or where you're going on vacation. When someone asks you about your vacation, you don't go into a 20 minute description and then set up a time to get together and walk them through the vacation brochure, which is the equivalent of what many people in MLM do.

Here's an example of how you do let people know that you're in business:

Prospect: "What do you do?"

Distributor: "I have a nutrition business. I do a lot of work with weekend warriors to help them recover faster."

That's it. You don't launch into a 20 minute presentation of talking about the business or products and trying to setup a meeting with the person. If the person has any interest, he'll ask a question or say something. If he doesn't, that's fine, too, because you just advertised your business and have one more person who knows what you're doing. You never know when that person may give you a referral or come back and ask a question.

The example we gave was a product focused one, geared toward getting customers. It's actually a partial example of our Personal Customer Endorsement. You'll notice it's very specific and focuses on a benefit rather spouting off facts or stats. If you're interested in learning more or creating your own, then check out our Personal Customer Endorsement course. It will walk you through the entire process of creating your own endorsement to let people know you're in business all the way through the customer acquisition process. We also have the

Personal Business Endorsement course that focuses on letting people know about the potential of starting their own business.

Do Market and Advertise Your Business!

You need to market and advertise your business so people who are actively looking for what you have to offer can find you. You can advertise your business with classified ads, YouTube video marketing, bandit signs, postcards, Facebook advertising, or your website on Google, to name a few. We've done all of those and then some. Part of becoming a Complete Networker is learning how to advertise your business in order to generate leads who are actually interested in hearing from you.

You have to walk before you can run. So before you can advertise, you need to master the basics. If you can't get a customer or distributor by talking with someone in your personal network, you're going to have a hell of a time doing it with advertising. Advertising is not a magical cure-all. It will magnify your abilities. If you're good at talking with people, you'll get good results with advertising. If you're horrible at talking with people, you'll get horrible results with advertising. If you're great at talking with people, you'll get great results with advertising. Get the point?

We constantly see new MLM distributors spend all this time and money on developing websites and ads when they have had zero success in their business! We're all for advertising to generate leads. We've spent hundreds of thousands of dollars over our careers on advertising to generate leads. We learned to walk before we learned how to run. It takes time to get really great at advertising. We also want to make sure you have balance in your business when it comes to building your business and spending time learning about advertising and marketing. Developing advertising and marketing skills takes money and time.

Do Participate In Lead or Traffic Cooperatives

The best way to leverage your time and money in regards to generating leads through marketing and advertising is by participating in lead or traffic cooperatives. To avoid any confusion, a lead and traffic cooperative is different from buying leads from a lead vendor. A lead and traffic cooperative is where people pool their money together to buy an advertisement or run a marketing campaign. This setup generally allows people to increase their buying power and also better advertising rates. Most importantly, it allows newer and less experience people to join a marketing campaign run by a successful and experienced leader or team.

Walking you through an example will help you understand lead and traffic cooperatives. In the previous chapter we described our entrepreneurship focused website, www.AntiSuitEntrepreneur.com. Pages on the websites offer free downloads, mentorship consultations and more information on becoming an entrepreneur. Once a month we allow people to buy a share of a traffic cooperative. Each share represents partial ownership of that month's marketing budget. For this example, let's assume 10 people each commit $100. 10 x $100 is $1,000. The $1,000 is the total marketing budget for the month. Each person will receive 10% of the leads and traffic that visit the website.

The people who opt in or buy the book become an immediate lead because they submitted their contact details. Other people will just visit without putting in their contact details; those people become tagged traffic. The website tags every visitor so if they come back in the future (up to 12 months away) and buy the book or opt in, the website will link them back to the original share owner. If this lead and traffic cooperative generates 100 leads and 1,000 tagged traffic visitors that means each person will receive 10 immediate leads and 100 people tagged to them. Tagging traffic has become increasingly important because fewer and fewer website visitors put in their contact details or buy something on the first visit. It's important to have a way to track them in the long run.

A lead and traffic cooperative doesn't guarantee you a certain number of leads or tagged traffic each month. You're not buying a certain number of leads, rather you're buying part of the performance of the marketing cooperative. At first glance this method throws some people for a loop. However, it's the best way to generate high quality leads. Rather than focusing on a certain number, the focus is on generating high quality traffic and leads. This system is best for you and your business. If the focus becomes generating a certain number of leads, then you'll get stuck in the same situation as you do with lead vendors.

Hopefully your leader or team has some sort of lead or traffic cooperative in which you can participate. If they don't, you'll need to create your own. You need leads and so will your future team.

Do Create a Website

Every business today needs a website. That's the bottom line. That includes you and your business! Your company's replicated website that you get as a distributor does not count. For a variety of reasons... they just stink. It's not easy or inexpensive to create an effective website for your MLM Business.

Websites need content. You have to figure out what content to put on your website. You can't use replicated websites where you fill in a few blanks and upload your image. You don't want to do what many in the MLM industry are doing with their "Fake 'Til You Make it - I'm an MLM Marketing Master Guru" crap. We could literally write a novel on those that don't work. We won't go into all the details, but trust us on this one.

You can't just put on your website, "I'm with company XYZ... and here are all the facts about it..." The vast majority of online advertisers (including Google and Facebook) don't allow websites like that. They will tell you that you can't advertise. And in some cases, as with Google, they will permanently ban you from ever advertising with them in the future. We're not saying we agree with that; but, those are the rules and it's best to play by the rules. Even more importantly, that type of website will not help you sign people up into your business. In fact, they'll do more harm than good!

People don't join network marketing companies because they are debt free and publicly traded on the stock exchange. Generally speaking, they join because they feel that the company and you can help them achieve their financial goals. MLM is a "financial vehicle" that can help take a person from his current financial situation to a better financial situation. The same is true for your product or service. People become customers because they want to receive the benefit of the product, whether that's better health, more energy, or whatever. This is true in all industries. People buy the benefit, not the features.

The way to accomplish this goal is with the concept of personal branding. Personal branding is built around you, your interests and your expertise. In reality, people are also joining you, not just your company. Personal branding allows people to relate with you and build a relationship with you. Personal branding is really built around the Develop step (as discussed earlier and covered in our Communication Course). Your website is really the ultimate tool for "building the bridge" from where your prospect is to where your company and MLM are.

You need two things for a Personal Branding website.

1) The "know how" of Personal Branding.

Learning and implementing a personal branding website take time and have a learning curve. But the investment is well worth it. Our Lead Generation course starts out with the concept of personal branding, so you can create your own brand. The course will take you through the entire process, step-by- step. It has over 100 videos that break down every aspect of Personal Branding and using your website to generate leads. It will walk you through everything from creating your concept, writing your eBook, setting up your website, creating email lists, advertising online, using it offline, and everything in between! You'll actually get to see how we created and maintain some of our other personal branding websites. It's a heavy duty course designed to get heavy duty results.

2) A website and marketing platform.

This is the technical side of your personal branding website. There's a lot to setting up your website. You have to determine what platform you're using, where to host it, how to design the site, plug in an email auto responder, put videos on your site, create capture pages, make it work on iPhones and iPads, and a 1,001 other things! Figuring out all the "techie stuff" is what causes most people to quit in frustration. They get lost in the process.

We grew tired of our downline wasting money and time on trying to figure everything out themselves. So we built our own website and marketing platform. Our system is 100% custom built and completely proprietary. No other MLM system out there is as complete as our system.

Over the years, we've invested over $1,000,000 in creating it. This isn't the typical system that MLMer's or affiliate marketers sell. The systems they sell are just replicated capture and sales pages. Our system is a fully functional one that allows you to build a website from the ground up, gives you all the tools you need to market and generate leads, and provides a contact management system to keep track of everyone. MLMCompletePackage.com and AntiSuitEntrepreneur.com were both built with this system.

We use the exact same tools that you and our downline have access to. Our goal was to build our dream system. We did that. And we're constantly improving it. Our system is so good that traditional small businesses have now started using it! Yes, we're heavily "plugging" our system and our course for personal branding. Why are we "plugging" our system? We're doing that because we've never seen a "good" course and/or system out there for network marketers. So, if we can make money off something that people really need and it helps them make money, that's just good business.

All the available systems out there don't really teach you how to market and build your business. They teach you how to sell the owner's products and system. While earning that affiliate commission may sound good, you're really hurting your business in the long run. We're not just talking about the disastrous results from the "Tale of 3 Network Marketers" story we told you earlier in this chapter.

The reason you're hurting your business is because you're not learning real marketing skills, which means you can never become truly self-sufficient. It's our goal to make you a real marketer. We want you to have the skills, so you can create websites, write copy, and generate leads on your own. Becoming a real and competent marketer was one of our goals years ago. We have an interesting story that drives home this point. While we were working on this book, Chris was reading a section of Chapter 2 out loud to Jason for a critique. After we were finished reading, someone came over and asked, "Did you guys write this?" We replied "yes."

He said, "I work in marketing and always tune out people's sales copy, but not yours. It actually grabbed my attention, and I kept wanting to hear more." After talking for a bit, it turned out that he worked for a very prestigious social media marketing management company in New York City that has accumulated many Fortune 500 clients. By the end of the conversation, he asked if we were available for work! We told him we really appreciated the offer, but we're just unemployable at this point. (Smile)

Guess where we learned all of our marketing skills? It's from our network marketing business building activities. If you don't use our system and course, make sure you're with a solid website and marketing platform and that you're also learning real marketing skills. We have a saying, "Sell you, not the guru!" If you do decide to utilize our system and course, we're looking forward to helping you build a strong MLM business and also become a real marketer.

Chapter 6
Get Organized

Staying organized isn't "sexy" or flashy, but it is essential to building a solid income in MLM. As Jason started mentoring Chris, it became apparent to Chris that Jason was extremely methodical in running his MLM business. Jason explained that when he ran the law firm, the constant pressure of a potential malpractice suit always lingered in the background. Missing a simple deadline for a client's court case could screw up the entire case and cause the client to miss out on hundreds of thousands of dollars of settlement income. If that scenario happened, the law firm could be sued for malpractice by their client and potentially be on the hook for all that money.

The law firm would represent hundreds of cases simultaneously and had dozens of employees managing different aspects of those cases. It's not hard to imagine how easy it would be for something to slip through the cracks. That's why the law firm was extremely organized and had a rigid process for handling every case. The law firm never once was sued for malpractice, which was quite an accomplishment. In fact, it had such a good reputation, that its employees were often called into other lawyers' malpractice lawsuits to testify. The organization and process not only kept the law firm out of hot water, but also allowed it to expand and become more profitable.

Fortunately, a lack of organization in your MLM business will not cause you to get sued for six or seven figures. However, it can cost you in distributors recruited, customers acquired, training your team effectively, and ultimately, impact your income. Many MLM distributors are at one extreme or another when it comes to this. They either have nothing and fly by the seat of their pants or spend so much time staying organized that they never build the business and get results! This chapter will focus on helping you get organized and creating a business building process.

Use a Contact Manager

Have you ever looked at how much time, money, and resources that successful businesses and professionals invest in developing, maintaining, and running their contact managers? Depending on their size, it's anywhere from a few hundred dollars a month (for a single sales professional) to millions of dollars a month (for larger businesses).

Why do they invest so much? Because they know it makes a difference to their bottom line. A recent study conducted by Nucleus Research concluded that companies using a contact manager earned $5.60 for every $1 they spent. They were more on top of their customers, contacts, and follow-ups and had a lot fewer "slip through the cracks." When you think about it, that isn't surprising.

However, many MLM distributors never take the time to get set up properly with a contact manager. Successful businesses are built by staying organized with a contact manager. They don't rely on a pile of sticky notes sitting on the desk! The first step to getting organized is to use a contact manager.

In 2009 we did a lead and traffic cooperative. The marketing was geared toward entrepreneurism and helping people find a home based business. This coop was extremely successful and helped many distributors recruit new distributors into their MLM organizations. As with any lead source, some people were ready to get started immediately and others were not. One of the distributors made sure he followed up with all the good people with whom he had connected. He ended up recruiting four new distributors... in 2012 and 2013! You read that correctly; because of his follow-up, he recruited four distributors three to four years after his initial contact with them.

We've had many similar stories over the years and every time other distributors hear about it, they want to know the secret. The secret is being organized! He was able to do this because he was organized with a contact manager and knew the communication steps that we outlined earlier in this book. It took him very little effort and time to follow-up with these people. He didn't follow-up for years with every single lead from the coop, rather he did so with the high quality people at appropriate time intervals.

How many distributors and customers have you missed out on because you dropped the ball on follow-up? One, two... dozens? It's a sobering reality check to think about.

A contact manager isn't just for your prospects. Use it for your current customers and downline distributors. Businesses and MLM distributors put so much effort into acquiring customers, but then drop the ball on basic customer service to turn them into long term and loyal customers! It doesn't take much time to do proper follow-up with your customers, if you're organized with a contact manager. Do at least one engagement once per month with each customer. An engagement is a phone call, voicemail, email, text message, Facebook message, or anything that has you engage with the person. This very simple approach will help you create long term customers.

When you engage your customers, do these two steps:

1. See how the person is doing with your product or service. How are things going? Do any updates or changes need to be made?
2. Share one relevant piece of information that further educates the person on your product or service. You know

what the person's interests or goals are, so share a piece of information that he will find relevant.

Despite what you may think, you don't need to have a conversation with the person to do these two steps. You can leave a 45 second voicemail that is incredibly effective. We have left many messages along these lines, "Hey Mr. Customer. Just wanted to touch base to make sure everything was good with product XYZ. Also, thought you would get a kick out of this... But so-so who is on 'Dancing with the Stars' is also using the products! I'll forward you an email with a write-up. If there's anything I can help you out with, give me a call."

Many customers will not call you back. That's fine. They are busy people with a thousand things going on. They will listen to your voicemail, appreciate the follow-up and learn something new about the company or product. These engagements add up over the long run.

Finding a Contact Manager

The previous chapter discussed the system that we developed. Our system actually started out as a contact manager and then grew into a marketing platform over the years. Jason knew the importance of staying organized with all of the prospects, so his first goal was to find a contact manager. There are many more options for contact managers than there were when we started our MLM businesses. All the contact managers he checked out would not cut it for the MLM industry because they were all built by people outside of the industry! He did find some systems promoted by MLM "gurus," but they were just rebranded third party systems. Using one of those contact manager systems would be the equivalent of "fitting a square peg in a round hole." Jason built a system for him and his team to use.

We could easily write a 300 page technical manual on creating a contact manager, but we don't want to put you to sleep. Here are a few important areas:

- It must have the ability to manage prospects, customers, and downline distributors. They also need to be separated. You don't want your customers getting emails intended for business prospects!
- It should be built around the MLM sales and communication process. You don't want the trying to "fit a square peg in a round hole" issue.
- It must be something that your team can duplicate. It has to work on all computer systems and devices.
- It needs the ability to have contacts automatically entered in from website capture pages.
- It must be able to transfer leads to other team members. Almost on a daily basis, we're transferring leads to distributors in our downline. As your business starts growing, you'll be glad you have this ability.

A common mistake distributors make is to put off getting organized until they start having success. Big mistake. You don't have success and then start doing what needs to be done for success. Success follows successful actions and habits. Act like a Complete Networker to become a Complete Networker. Hopefully the distributor's story about sponsoring four distributors will spur you into taking time and getting set up with a contact manager. If your team or upline doesn't have one in place, then check out the one we developed specifically for MLM distributors at www.MLMCompletePackage.com

Chapter 7
Become a Complete Networker

If our "business common sense" approach to MLM resonated with you, then it's time to become a Complete Networker. A word of caution: don't learn the skills and then get side-tracked. We see so many people learn new things that help them, but after a while they forget what they learned. The question is how can you become a Complete Networker and then make sure you stay on track, so you build a successful MLM organization. This chapter will walk you through a series of helpful points.

Get On Board with your Network Marketing Company

You must "get on board" with your network marketing company. If you don't believe in your network marketing company, then becoming a Complete Networker is going to be a waste of time. Many people ask us what they need to do to get on board with their network marketing. Our response is simple: Do you believe in the company? Do you really believe in it? Would you take the product or use the service even if you did **not** do the business? Be honest! Finally, if you pass that test, then in our opinion, your company must pass the "customer test" discussed earlier. Do the calculation at the end of Chapter 1 to find out what your compensation plan will pay you for getting customers. Hopefully building a customer base makes financial sense. If it doesn't, then you need to make sure you have a plan clearly laid out for how you can make the business work to meet your goals. Throughout this book, we have made our position clear on how important having a customer base is for the long term success of your business.

If you can't get on board with your company, then please don't turn your back on this business model. We completely believe in the network marketing business model, if it's set up correctly (such as getting paid properly for building a customer base) and its product or service resonates with you. Although we cannot get into all the details to consider when selecting an MLM company in this book, we will tell you that the "common killer" of an MLM opportunity is its lack of customer compensation. It's that critical to your long-term success. That said, if you can't get on board with your network marketing company, then it's time to find one with which you are compatible.

If you are going to embark on that journey, then you need to learn how to select an MLM opportunity; notice we didn't say "how to select an MLM company." You can find the best company in the world, but it doesn't mean it's the best opportunity. A solid MLM company is a part of what makes a good MLM opportunity. Don't embark on this journey without reading our book, *How To Select An MLM Opportunity*. You can find it at http://www.MLMCompletePackage.com/HowToSelect

Learn How to Get Customers

Once you have "gotten on board" with your network marketing company, then it's time to start learning how to get customers. You can seek out any source that resonates with you on getting customers. Your company, upline / team, or other sources may have training that helps you get customers. We don't care how you learn; you just need to learn how to do it and make it happen. On our website, we have a training course to teach you how to get customers. The course is called Customer Endorsement. Use our course or whatever course that makes sense to you and get this step done. We just want you to build a customer base. Getting customers is absolutely critical to the long term success of your business.

Master Sales & Communication

You need to learn a sales and communication process that you can apply to your business. It's probably obvious that better communicators will get more customers and recruit more distributors, but this process isn't just to use with prospects. Becoming a better communicator will also be used with your downline, crossline, and upline. Your ability to communicate with people will make or break your business. As mentioned earlier, find communication and sales training that is focused on MLM. There are numerous sales training courses available, but there are not a lot that focus on sales under the umbrella of a network marketing business. That's why we created our Communication course. We welcome you to use our training;but, again, just be sure to find something that helps you become a better communicator.

Start Training Your Downline

Once you have figured out how to get customers and improve your communication skills, your customer base and number of distributors in your organization will grow. You need to know how to train those distributors. Training is a complicated process that is often over simplified. Training people effectively is another misunderstood area in the network marketing industry. Training your downline depends on your ability to build the business. If you cannot build the business (getting customers or recruiting downline), then it's hard to train others. You need to learn the common pitfalls when training people. How much time do you spend with people? Who do you spend time with? Are you doing too much or too little? These are all questions distributors deal with. That's why we created our Train Your Team course. Our own downline needed something that answered these questions. Whatever you do, you need to get some insight on training your team.

Get a Contact Manager

You need a contact manager. Period. We highly recommend you use a contact manager that is built for the MLM industry. Check with your upline and company first to see if a contact manager is available. If there isn't a contact manager available, then look at the one we created (and use ourselves on a daily basis) at www.MLMCompletePackage.com/CompleteNetworker/System.

Lead Generation

Everyone wants the magical lead source. As we discussed earlier, in the long term, you need to build a brand and eventually a website. As you probably could see from what we discussed earlier, setting up a website (not the technical part, but the actual brand, theme and content) is a very daunting task. Building your brand is something you should work toward. Meanwhile, participating in a traffic and lead cooperative is a great way to gain new prospects. The problem is that most organizations in network marketing don't have the "know-how" to run successful traffic and lead cooperatives.

As we wrote this book, the inability for the majority of distributors to participate in a traffic and lead cooperative kept nagging at us. We know that leads are vital in building a successful MLM organization. While the Lead Generation course we created is a fantastic resource for building your brand and generating leads in the long term, we wanted to help you get leads in the short term. To truly offer the Complete Package we felt we had to operate within our belief in what we are doing; we had to offer you everything that we use or it wouldn't be the Complete Package.

Earlier in the book, we discussed how we run lead and marketing coops off of www.AntiSuitEntrepreneurs.com. People who complete the entire Complete Package training and become a Complete Networker will have the privilege of participating in our cooperatives. You may be wondering why you would have to go through the Complete Package training in order to participate. Put yourself in our shoes. We've put a tremendous amount of resources into the Anti Suit Entrepreneur and also have it built around our brand. We're putting our reputations on a limb in many ways.

We're trying to provide you the Complete Package, while also protecting our Anti Suit Entrepreneur brand. You must completely understand our philosophy on building a network marketing business through proper communication before you can represent our Anti Suit Entrepreneur brand. Anyone who is calling leads from the lead and traffic cooperative will be representing our brand. The easiest way for people to learn our philosophy is to go through the Complete Package and to become a Complete Networker.

One important point about using the Anti Suit Entrepreneur website, book, and lead cooperative is that they are generic. It doesn't mention our company. It doesn't even mention network marketing, except at the end of the last chapter. The last chapter sends people to the "How We Started" video. The video explains how network marketing helped us get started in entrepreneurship. It's done very professionally and in a way that someone new to business can understand. It's a great bridge for your network marketing business.

A Special Offer for Becoming a Complete Networker

We believe the Complete Package and the Anti Suit Entrepreneur marketing cooperative can be a game changer for many distributors in MLM. We've put together a special package for the readers of this book who are interested in getting the Complete Package and becoming a Complete Networker. To learn more visit www.MLMCompletePackage.com/CompleteNetworker/CompletePackage Make sure you use the link from this book, for a special offer only through this book.

Don't Get Side-Tracked

The biggest problem with network marketers is that they are bombarded with the newest lead generation tricks, the next script that will change their business, and the next "walk over hot coals" event that's going to change their business. They get side-tracked. If our "business common sense" philosophy resonates with you, then get plugged int o free training. One way to help you avoid getting side tracked is by getting a regular dose of "business common sense."

Every week, we post new trainings that answer the day-to-day questions we get, new topics that come up, or clarifications on the training and courses on our website. We post them in three different formats:

- Free Blog & Newsletter
- Free YouTube Training
- Free Podcast

Regardless of which you choose, you'll get the same training. It just depends on what format resonates the most with you. Some people like to read blogs; others like to watch YouTube videos; maybe you are a podcast person. The point is, we have whatever format fits your personality. Just get plugged in, so you don't get side-tracked.

"Business Common Sense" for Your Business

We sincerely hope that our message of "business common sense" helps you with building your MLM Business. Our goal is to instill the "business common sense" mantra into you. The manta can be a constant reminder on how to build your business. It should also raise a red flag when you start hearing the "cheesy" MLM training and help you stay on track for building your business.

Helping people in the MLM industry is a labor of love for us because we have gained so much over the years from building our MLM businesses. We want to see you and others have the same success. If we can ever help, please contact us through www.MLMCompletePackage.com/CompleteNetworker/Connect. That is a special page we created that is only accessible to readers of this book. We wish you well in your endeavors and sincerely hope you apply what you have learned here.

www.ingramcontent.com/pod-product-compliance
Lightning Source LLC
Chambersburg PA
CBHW070939210326
41520CB00021B/6965